On Top of my Game

by

Johnny W. Jackson III

Order this book online at www.trafford.com
or email orders@trafford.com

Most Trafford titles are also available at major online book retailers.

Print information available on the last page.

ISBN: 978-1-4669-1003-4 (sc)
ISBN: 978-1-4669-1002-7 (hc)
ISBN: 978-1-4669-1004-1 (e)

Library of Congress Control Number: 2011963405

Trafford rev. 09/07/2016

 www.trafford.com

North America & international
toll-free: 1 888 232 4444 (USA & Canada)
fax: 812 355 4082

-Dedicated-to my heavenly Father (Thanks for making me a strong brother)

-To Latrece M. Townsend (I was thinking about you when I was putting this book together . . . You are the best of the best)

Section 5

Section 6

Section 1

 A Sista

I need a sista who is family but not blood
A sista who shows you her world in her eyes.
A sista who dreams of places to go that I only imagine about going.
Telling her brother tales of her future and why the world is going to need her.
A sista that has seen her brother before but hasn't met him until years later.
One that knows her brother cares about her no matter how far they're apart.
A sista that describes love as a "perfect timing"
The timing is perfect because family finds each other.
I need a sista who wants a brother to show her she is not alone in this world.
A sista who likes family photos and sees herself smiling in each one.
A sista who just wanted a brother to look after her and her heart.

 I Need

I need that good love that strong love
that Mary J. Blige I need to be happy love.
I need that fire love that burns my heart as you keep on
feeding me cupids arrow.
I need that love that taste as good as grandma's tasty 7-up cake.
Well not that good but something with both feet and a toenail in it.
Not that skin deep love but let's just say did you ever hear that
saying
"When I cry you cry multiplied by two" why two?
Because the world is what we see in our eyes and it takes two of us
to help each other open them.
I need that love girl, thats deep down in my soul that combines with me.
Yeah that's what I need.

All in a Dream

Sitting here imagining you next to me
wondering if these words leave footprints
and not sketches in your heart.
Looking at your eyes and how they match
the tone of your smile.
Holding you in my arms wishing this dream
will last forever.
Looking at how tasty your lips look and would
you mind if I tasted them forever.
Cuddling up feeling the embrace of my hugs.
Will I ever get the chance to show you the true
meaning of happiness?
Seeing through the mist of the clouds holding hands
going through life as one. Always putting you beside
or above me and never below me. Shedding tears of joy every time
we meet, showing you there is no one better.
Knowing this girl brings something special to my heart
and my life.
Relieving you of all distractions only putting positive
thoughts in your head and me at the same time.

Beautiful Black Woman

Beautiful black woman, my beautiful black woman
Queen of my soul
The one I live for and the one I put first
Mother of my heart and my constant everything
Pretty deep coconut eyes and honey tasting skin
Ebony essence
The one I must hear and see to breathe
The one I must have
Tear drop smile
Romantic thoughts are forever with me and you
The faith that maybe I can hold her one day and forever
Two people two minds
One love
Testimony of my beautiful black woman

♣ | Feelings on Paper

Watching TV as it watches me.
Sitting here writing on paper telling it
everything I want it to know.
Slow dancing with my feelings as it
walks around you, as she is a part of my world.
Each day we step into a new kind of love but
instead of going with the song her name is now my last.

 Can I

Where should I start?
Can I walk with you to class?
I'll carry your books as you hold my words.
A statement that was prepared at sight and conceived with thy eyes.
Only difference is when I give your books back I still have your heart which I'm keeping.
Can I open the door for you? Are you in?
I'm talking about my mind, Are you in?
Can I pay for the meal?
I know I don't have to ask but independence is written all over your attitude
and that's why I researched, looked up and approached that line.
That line of you not having to settle.

Section 2

Fall

I wonder why they call this season fall
Is it because of the leaves falling or us falling together
The temperature is falling but not before you start liking me
Holding your face against mine
Are you still red in the face?
Look at the sky the clouds are moving with us
Does that mean were getting closer to marriage or separation?
Each day brings one or the other closer
Are you ready for it?
The air is falling on us, take cover because each breath
brings a longer journey of walking and then sprinting
The wind is pushing us this way does that mean we're suppose
to fall this way or naturally?
I still like this season even if fall is two steps away

That Feeling

The feeling of being loved is like no other.
It's the sound of a drummer loosening up in your heart.
Together the thought of sharing worlds follow us,
not knowing that we live in the same one.
My poem is your dream, so does it make it mine too?
The only feeling that surrounds you when you see me is
the growth of me and the stars that are below me.
Waking up to it and praising it.
The feeling that stays at its peak and I still have
to climb it even higher just to show off.
If you're smiling now, I guarantee you will be when I jump down.
I know nothing intimidates your path but the next level. I meant
the one with me.

 Empty

A pretty girl stood in front of me and I let her get away.
I traveled to see her through the toll, but I never had exact change.
A girl that should receive happiness but doesn't.
I pray everyday that she does, months overlap and so do my words.
Low self-esteem followed and I had to scratch through the braids.
Ten is the proper word to call her and I was too slow on giving those given
reasons.
Mailed but not sealed, the words leaked out on its destination.
Who makes her feel this way?
A girl that criticizes herself to bring herself down.
I tell myself that isn't real and I won't believe it.
Her compliments come from me, a friend, one person looking through the back window of an outside family.
Flowers that she receives and a reaction she is not sure to take.
I was trying to help strengthen her mind and I was taken out of hers.
My best friend, who made me see a ten, the first double-digit number and the last one I met.
The one who had all my numbers and memories had made our relationship a memory.
I have run on empty with no more memories to create in this indescribable friendship.

♣ | Too Deep

Hold my hand and crawl with me.
What is the possibility of this relationship?
Maybe we can grow into an inseparable romance.
Reality has no boundaries.
Let's talk about why we are here . . . and where we can go.
Thoughts of us become new subjects to the world.
Look outside our kingdom is waiting for us.
It's the year of raining smiles.
When I'm here happiness is unlimited.

The Sharpness of us

My heart has spoken . . . The sum of it all
is the sky is falling in your hands.
Maybe that's why I feel the embrace of it.
Just last year we met in that vacant season.
The mind of being God's son.
You don't have to pay the toll,
it's already taking its task. Damn we created
a monster. Between us it's more like it never
rains on our parade.
Remember today friend's becoming the best of us.
The theory of smiling cooked with a pinch of tucking you in through
tomorrow, which becomes today and then tomorrow again.
I guess the world has found its peace right here.
No put your hand here . . . yea right there.

♣ | 1st Grade Love

What you thought a Romeo can't start at an early age?

She was a quiet pretty girl with a big smile. Talking usually ends in a hug and a kiss goodbye. Taking her out was seeing her at school, like the classroom to be exact; and let me tell you I was too faithful to my class.

We told each other that love was in the air and we started breathing it in.

Now it hits the heart. Touching and kissing with recess in mind. That was our thing under the bridge. We didn't know what we were doing.

We were having school ourselves. Writing notes that ended in crooked words that we learned that day.

Our body language took over and those words came... "I love you," and we did to a first grader's point of view, right behind candy and chocolate milk.

Section 3

 Come

The water is over our head
shall we move or lay in the fall of it.
The sprouting of a new forest,
you know our backyard the one
we grew up in.
The thought of slamming the door
of our new house, not yet our home
until we seal it with a few more slams.
This ring I share with you and the kiss that seals it with my breath.

Come to me . . . I can't keep these thoughts
to myself. I want you
close. They say a scent is airborne and that
I can't see it. I don't agree.
Why . . . what does love smell like?
I guess it depends on what you think it is.
I can smell it from across the room and
your eyes just signed off on that.
Come and live the same prayer with me.
It's just my thoughts waiting for my eyes to open . . . come and
help me see it.

🍀| Slow Storm

The water is un-breathable and
the shower is underneath my head.
If you saw a puddle on a sidewalk
with my reflection, would you like to know
how deep it is?
Jump in . . . it was your moisture from your thoughts
of me. The fog is growing in the air and the
dampness of it appears on my lips,
my hand . . . my skin. Fog is everywhere and
since you created it, my lips is the first thing
you thought of. The smooth rain takes our breath away.
It's been going on for about a day now . . . that day feels
like today.
Stay for the storm and the drizzle
and I'll bring the thunder and lightning.
It's more than a change of weather.
Everytime you come around, I can do that. Now are you glad the
weather man told you not to bring an umbrella.
Come I'll hold you through this storm, fast or slow, steady or light.

♣ | Masterpiece

Make-up and the smell of natural beauty.
The beginning of my selfishness mixed
with the pursuit of my second happiness.
The dime that someone dropped and the
same one that I stepped under.
You asked me why . . . answer of confetti
Hold this bond and watch it grow over me.
This is too real, playground dreams that
only a few get to experience.
Maybe that's why I fell on one knee that night
and we're here now and tomorrow.
The steps that became leaps of joy.
So while I'm running, I'll grab that picture
for our living room that I promised you along
with that same feeling from that white winter
day we met. So the smell of natural beauty without make-up
because nothing about her is made up . . . its all true.

♣ | My Other Half

The reflection of my heart is standing outside the mirror.
My christian sister with the same father.
Honestly I knew you were here,
I just didn't know when I was going to touch you
outside of the family reunion.
A feeling of being born, but it's not a sight for
sore eyes but more like a swan for a dove's beauty.
The thing that matters most in the beginning of the
relationship and the harder it can get if we allow others to lift up
our bond.
Our connection is too strong . . . my other half
the other side of my hand and my heart. You look at half and see
the presence of both.

♣| Token

The toll . . . I paid it ever since I found you.
I should have had an I pass, but I did not know I would keep
passing through here for you.
I passed the toll many times and I was wondering if
I was going to cross your path.
No accident on me being here at different skies of the year.
I am like a man of much strength and when it comes to you
I feel like carrying the world is not enough.
Take this token, pocket it and never spend outside of the
toll is what she told me. Look this way . . . each time you see
my teeth you know I'm here for you. Next time you
will see even more teeth. I always keep it real
the only game I play is trying to make it to your heart without
pressing continue.
One of the pawns told me how to get next to the queen and
I will . . . now king me and lets go get something to eat. This day I
stood beside you and offered you a
token of my heart, along with a cloud. All you have to do is feel it
up with things that we can do.

Graffiti

I spray painted our name all over the town with our faith.
Our faith of growing and symbolizing why we are here.
This time next week the bridges and trains will have all been
spray painted. The world has to know about us right. I get mail from
across the world . . . I guess my message has gotten to them.
Graffiti, the power of words, that's almost like
saying bloody-mary three times in the mirror.
Say it . . . I dare you. I sprayed it with a can on this day
and she signed it with hand prints on that day.
Graffiti has multiple feelings, mostly on the inside of our house.
Trust me we didn't just move in it . . . It's all on the floor and
bedroom. Wait . . . you get the idea. I've been after her since
I knew I had the power to leave it all over town. Last week next
month I guarantee Graffiti was on my mind.

Section 4

Take Notes

My palm is sweating from holding your hand.
I can never get too old for that to happen.
I can't let go what's a part of me.
I feel like all the seasons are in me, but with so
many of them passing . . . I can't figure out which
one was the best of our lives. A pretty face is what
I dreamed of and now God has blessed me with a
life that doesn't end. The moment it rains is the
moment I cover the bed spread over you. I provide
and push for the best . . . maybe that's why I went for you and
helped provided you with the best. I took those notes growing
up and I used them to help me go after what I wanted when I got
older . . . you.

Thinking of You . . . Often

It's the same beginning with the same theme.
The difference of making your lips sit up, that's
how you know the sun is going to shine today.
Maybe it's the sight of happiness in your eyes and
the word love in mine.
Nervousness can carry a feeling that goes both ways
and seeing you brings it out. The realest a man can describe our
friendship at the top of its and my vocabulary.
I miss your presence in my face. Side stepping the truth
on the word apart. It's the word that I see and being a part of you
gives me a good vibe.
The growth of an undefined term, but I just take dreams
one cloud at a time. I agree with the time change, especially when
it comes to the seasons changing. For some reason I always find
you in the same one.
Out of my hands and into yours . . . don't close them.

🍀| She Can Dance!

The floor is moving to the beat. A mysterious but sexy dancer is calling me out.

Her body is moving with the bass, I can feel it in my chest every time she moves on me. I look up and see her dancing with the stars and the moon seems to be resting

peacefully. It must know who's performing tonight. A circle has formed around her. I believe she has the gift of having

everyone's eyes on her.

She's in her own world with her own desires. No wonder I couldn't find her,

I was busy looking in my own. The only thing that is better than her moves

is her beauty and the fountain of youth is in her eyes.

The spotlight is on her; all ears are to the rhythm of her feet.

I must admit this girl has soul…mine and hers.

Seeing her makes me want to move my feet, maybe I should stop daydreaming and move my lips to ask her for a dance.

 The Wick

Match it up and sharpen the air with her scent.
The contents within the glass are flammable.
I'm not smoking, but my lungs are filled with her
waxy perfume. She is in my house but more on my schedule. I lit
her yesterday and today I watched her hold that same flame. It can
stand a breath upon it.
Specifically mine! Many times I felt the heat and each time I can
tame it. I never put it out because I sleep better and sometimes I
even stay up because the light is always in my background.
That's how you know it's a special night . . . the candle comes out
along
with the taste of that aroma that soon becomes my oxygen.
A few hours later the candle starts sweating wax from the high
temperature that is created. My match is strong and my strike is
even stronger, maybe that's why the glass is melting from the
flame within because she
knows I'm getting ready to strike a match.

 Pursue

To pursue is to try but with her it's natural. As if I needed to be a part of her life, like I was lucky to cross her path, like I had picked a four leaf clover out of the ground. She was unique to the eye that gave her personality a more reason to be self-conscious.

I didn't know what to look at but I did know what to look for. She reminded me of a winter breeze that made my skin num when she touched me.

I had never pursued a girl like I had with her, almost like I knew who my other half would be. Though she is a friend it never felt like it. I went through every wrong turn that was given to me to stay in reach of her.

I have the whole world to look forward to and I'm hoping to have her to do that with.

🍀| I can't describe it

You are an amazing person to me. I can't describe the beauty of your makings.

You make me wanna . . . I can't describe it, although I can touch up on it.

Maybe something out of a waterfall that keeps sprouting the purest water.

Something that was made to be in the sky, kind of like a sparkler that I can

hold in my hand and aim upward at the night. Something you have to see . . . a lunar eclipse

to remind you it does exist. Almost like learning to ride your first bike its big to you and even

bigger to your parents taking the picture. That feeling can't be replaced.

It's more of a cotton candy flavor that even as an adult you still have to taste it.

Yea it's something like that. Now remember I just touched up on it.

I still can't really describe it.

Section 5

♣ | Stone Park

At the pool hall I waited, didn't have any doubt that you weren't going to show. You know it was your neighborhood that I wanted to introduce my guys to. You had that kind of affect where I wanted you to get more involved in my life. My mom would be the next person after my friends. They were just the beginning and she was towards the end, that's if you make it that far. You walked in with your girl, I was speechless it's like I only see gorgeous up close and personal when you're around. Braided up you were, my friend stated that girl is wifey. I had to agree just looking at you built up my confidence that you wanted to hang out with me and the goons. Teaching you how to hold the pool stick, it was a scene out of booty call. The smell of you just kidnapped me; regardless of how good I was, I wanted you to win. My friends were impressed... I was more in capturing the center of our friendship. A memory I hold in my hand. When it was time to go only me and you wanted to grab something to eat. I guess my friend and your friend wasn't ready to hold hands yet, but that didn't stop us from holding each others hand.

Wait for her

I was told to be patient for you. Like I'm supposed to stop the days I was living for her. It was hard, but God knew who I wanted. I didn't want to buy a calendar but I had to. I even hung it in my room counting the days I haven't talked to you.

You wonder how I knew you would be the one, easy, God told me, he told me to be patient. He placed you in my mind at different times in different scenes. I couldn't forget you, God wouldn't let me.

He placed me next to you for a reason. We talked once a year and it was driving me crazy. I was told to wait. I was told to pray for her and that she needed that more than she needs me now. I had to bless and encourage her with good things from a distance.

What you wasn't telling me I was feeling spiritually. Then I knew I had to wait and let God work things out. He told me in the mean time not to waste my life, but make myself better. When the time comes everything that I wanted will fall into place including her.

♣| *Not so Ordinary*

You ever met anyone like me...a guy can't be picked apart, but can be picked out of a crowd. Created with a purpose created for you. The day I met you, God smiled, he knew the relationship and how it could change and now he gets to watch it play out first hand. You should bring your parents out with us I'm sure they would want to see what world their daughter is living in. Now that I have your attention you may be seated. I'll pick up dinner while you read the last verse. This time the honeymoon is on me dipped in the purple sky as we look out the window to our next palace. This is the reason why I'm in your arms . . . not so ordinary and neither is our path. The quietest in school and voted most to speak my mind once graduated. Get out of my way I'm going in too fast to your lips better yet make it a haymaker. Test the water and get in, the ph scale is tilted towards 1. Damn you're dangerous and so is thee.

Something Different

It's kind of like this . . . trust goes both ways and so does our relationship. More like a bond, a savings bond that won't be cashed even after it has fully matured. Fully cooked we prefer charcoal over propane.

The original flavor with the two sides on the side to make it a complete family a complete meal. A fresh coat of paint to keep the relationship going.

Same color just more I love you's and teenage scenarios. We're an item not something you can pick up at the store. Although I will be there to help pick you up as you would do the same.

Let's try something different tonight, how about no seat belts in the bedroom. You don't have to smile yet I didn't even open the door yet. We are something different but still adjacent to each other.

The fact is we will never let go or give up but we are open to being something different.

♣ | Return the Favor

This paperback tells you a different side of me

and these words tell you that I found a different side of you.

I'm just saying you made me feel this way, made

me write this book and now its time to

return the favor. Am I making you do things

differently as well. I mean last week you told me you felt

inspired and unique and that I had something to

do with it. I told you we will get through this together.

One door closes another one opens. The windows

are fogging up and I can't roll them down or maybe I don't want

to. I call it second hand conversation. It's more

deadlier than the original conversation. I wonder what else I can

do to show you your true self. Maybe an endless

supply of support will help. I want you to be the best and feel the

best. I want you to know that you're with the best.

I want to help you grow with me and in this world. I'm glad we

can do more for each other outside of our home.

♣ | On Top of my Game

On top of my game is apart of me. The guy who sent you those flowers and then heard how you got them at home on your way back to work from lunch. Man god works in mysterious ways.

Look at this with a magnifying glass.

No matter the small things I do for you for some reason you always see it big. Kind of like remembering something you told me a decade ago.

You're like ancient china that friends always compliment on. I usually don't brag but they knew about you before you were even sure about me.

One of the few to ring the door bell when picking you up. One of the few to let you drive the whip. Do you see the shirt you ruined, so quick to get me out of it. Now I have to keep it because you bought it for me.

Like a directory guide, you are there, but you need to be here. On top of my game for years and it will only get higher as I continue to grow.

Section 6

Whatever it takes

Like a river, I'll jump in if I knew the future. Better yet, I'll dive in if it was with you. I need you here with me on this street. Now turn around is this the house you wanted.

Whatever it takes to touch you to see you in the background of my mirror. To see you and me in the family tree. Better we walk together then to leave one behind.

You like to put your lips together. I like to take them apart with mine. You ever seen the smoke settle from a kiss. I need that.

My light needs to shine brighter. I need your electricity to power my life. Now and forever whatever it takes. I need you to prescribe me your love . . . chewable please.

The forecast is a hail storm all week. Maybe we should leave the bedroom for awhile. I need that all year. A woman that's going to make me do whatever it takes to make her my wife.

 Congested

Its been months since I seen that movie. The one you took me to when I had a girl who believes I left her for you.
Its more of you took me by the hand and showed me what life would be like with you.

So it's only right to say I was there when your boyfriend wasn't. If it happened my way, my ex would've been right, I would've left her for you.

Once I met you I was congested with you...my eyes, ears, nose, mouth and chest were all congested with your beauty, voice, smell, taste and heart thanks to you. No other woman can touch your level, the one above the top floor.

It's like tying a tie to tight that I can't breath. The only problem was I'm not sure you would've left him for me. We never talked about it, just our company with each other was enough as I thought.

Along with the companies we talked about working for years later. I'm single now but I'm hoping by the time you get this that will change. This message, this poem, this book...it's all one.

♣ | Endless Days

Lower the bridge so we can pass. Our schedule lets us spend more time than planned or maybe it was planned but out of our reach. Sometimes the days rollover to the 25th hour. Like our night ended after dinner, but our morning opened with a walk on the beach, which is something usually done after dinner.

I counted a total of 11 of these endless days this morning. I wonder how it would be if we lived together. That's the direction it's going in. The same way as the sun, funny we started out in the direction of the moon some hours ago. You can add another one to make it a total of 12.

It's a scene out of a book, this one without any pictures just the ones I color in your mind. If I started jogging down a one-way street it will eventually turn into a two-way street. Thanks for joining me I couldn't have done it alone. Endless days turn into memories that just keep extending. It's like our year only had 114 days and this year it look like it maybe shorter.

♣ | On Top of my Game Remix

Usually is not in my vocabulary unless it's me usually taking you out.

This week the Signature Room next week a piece of paper will be asking for ours.

Relax I got this. You got a man who can talk you into a smile. A man who keeps pushing you higher on the swing as you reach the top.

A man of God to go along with a queen of spades, the toughest queen of them all.

Can you turn the TV down my heart has something to say.

I'm here with you, us a magnet, as a combination that can't be turned in any direction.

Handsome I am and on top of my game I is. Solve the puzzle, you can't define me, a challenge to your mind.

Tell you what...I'll even you see me in 2-D. In the box above circle other.

Better yet, ask my ex, I mean she took my mom out in the first month she met me just to see how something like me was created.

Sincere to myself and sincerely yours...your man.

 Rematch

Turn the clocks back, lets relive the night. I think I pulled a back muscle. I have to work in the morning but I want a rematch. I guarantee you I won't lose this time. Will see if you even get to throw in the towel. Sit up, no handicapped matches, I want to put you on your back and then your stomach. I'm sure you took enough punishment from this side already. I mean I got combos for hours. New rule, the whole house is the ring, but we're lying on the dining room table already so I'm sure you already knew that. Desert is served which is probably why you won the last match because of the buffet. I mean even super heroes take at least one night off. Now like I promised I'll bring the world to you in one night. Oh don't worry you will be soaking in the Red Sea. You might want to pick up a few souvenirs so you can say that you were there and then was able to leap to another continent. When it's over I'll go out and pick up a globe that way I can show you what part of the world you ran from.

♣| I Already Knew

Today is not the day, but tomorrow is. See I can vision the future so I can tell you before it happens that I will be asking your dad for your hand in marriage.

It will lead up to me proposing to you. I do have a third eye and it can stay focus even when it blinks occasionally from water getting into it.

It's more than just feelings it's a gift that I was told to keep under the tree. No lamp around just a bible around that rubbed on me when I opened it.

Believe me when my heavenly father tells me things and it's the same way when I close my eyes. From my lips to yours, can I trust you with this Intel. The longer you believe, the same language we will speak.

Believe me, because we're standing here today and yesterday you couldn't speak to me. The signs I see are for me to vision and to eventually put in your vocabulary. Just like I knew one day you would be reading this.

I created my own path and I witnessed the dust try to cover it up. It later retracted when it finally gave in to witnessing my shoeprints cannot be covered up.

I can see the future and the signs on the interstate, which is showing me billboards of us being together.

♣ | Supporting Cast

I think about where we started from, to where I am now if it wasn't for your support. Someone who separated the term friend to best friend. I stood by your side through all the things you discovered you didn't want to be.

I listened to everything you told me, some of it I didn't agree with, but you always had my support. I remember I told you the plan that I kept sketching over and over in my head. I remember I kept my word, the one I mentioned back in community college. I did everything I told you I was going to do. Look at you, a designer and I must say my interior hasn't been the same since I met you. But now I'm visioning it happen years after you first mentioned it to me. I'm honored to have known you during the outline period. I'm glad you were able to hear my plans and support me in my contract years.